A Melody of Silent Desires

In the silence of the night,
A chorus springs to life, what a sight!
A snail composes quite a tune,
As a shy skunk twirls by the moon.

The fireflies blink in rhythm neat,
As the grasshoppers tap their feet,
In a band that's not too shy,
Except when the fox walks by.

A songbird hums low and sweet,
While the rabbits lose their beat,
As a raccoon strums a line,
With clumsy paws, but feeling fine.

Thus they play in shared delight,
A melody of wild, free flight,
Underneath the starlit skies,
With laughter echoing surprise.

Tapestry of Leafy Aspirations

In a world so green and lush,
Where leaves join in a playful hush,
A fox struts with elegant flair,
Wearing socks, his feet laid bare.

The vines tickle the birds above,
As they sing of mischief and love,
A caterpillar polka-steps,
While a bear clumsily preps.

Amidst the roots, a dance is spun,
Where laughter echoes through the fun,
The rise and fall of leafy dreams,
Float like sweet and silly schemes.

Nature's party, without a care,
With joys that bubble in the air,
The tapestry unfolds each night,
With giggles that make the stars shine bright.

Soft Echoes of the Moonlit Path

On a path where shadows play,
Bats come out to dance and sway,
A turtle breaks into a jig,
While a hedgehog wears a wig.

Oh, the trees are quite the sight,
Swinging gently in the night,
With whispers of secrets shared,
By critters who just don't care.

The fireflies blink their lights,
In delightful dizzy flights,
While the owls hoot in tune,
To mischiefs 'neath the moon.

A gathering of glee and fright,
Following the path so bright,
Funny tales spun all around,
With joy in every sound.

Murmurings from the Hidden Thicket

In a thicket full of cheer,
Where the squirrels sip their beer,
A frog croaks out a tune,
While a cat plays the bassoon.

The owls wear tiny hats,
Dance with curious acrobats,
While rabbits tap their feet,
To the rhythm of the beat.

A hedgehog sings in glee,
Underneath the old pine tree,
And all the critters laugh,
At nature's merry musical staff.

The crickets join the fun,
Underneath the glowing sun,
In a concert that won't stop,
Till the laughter makes them hop.

Echoes among the Twisted Roots

Down in the depths where the roots intertwine,
Is a turtles' meeting, sipping on brine.
They chuckle at tales of their slow, steady race,
While laughter erupts from the mossy old space.

The shadows leap and the beetles groove,
In their underground party, there's nothing to prove.
"Who's fastest here?" They all sing out loud,
As worms wiggle by, feeling supremely proud.

Each twist in the roots tells a giggling yarn,
Of critters dressed fancy, picking at corn.
The air is thick with mischief and jest,
As the laughter from below rises high with the rest.

So if you should wander and hear the delight,
Remember the secrets that spark in the night.
Among twisted roots where friendships consume,
Echoes of laughter in earthy perfume.

Murmurs of the Swaying Boughs

The branches sway and gossip with flair,
About a fox who thinks he's debonair.
"Look at my tail, isn't it grand?"
But a raccoon rolls eyes, saying, "Oh, please, man!"

In this leafy chatter, the critters unite,
As the ants march by, each one feels just right.
A crow tells a joke from high on his perch,
While the fawns pause, mid-licking a birch.

Beneath the boughs, the laughter resumes,
As the flowers shake with comical blooms.
A beetle spins tales of heroic delight,
Of a snail who won an all-night-long flight.

So listen closely as the woodwinds play,
Nature's own ramble, where laughter won't stray.
With murmurs that tickle and joys that ignite,
In this swaying world, everything feels right!

Secrets in the Whispering Breeze

The breeze confides in the tickling pine,
"Why was that tree wearing a funny design?"
The leaves all giggle, their laughter in flight,
As squirrels debate if the joke's out of sight.

A frog croaks bass with a humorous flair,
While butterflies join in a swirling affair.
Each puff of wind carries tales so absurd,
Of a stoic old toad trying to be heard.

The flowers blush, their petals unfold,
With secrets of wisdom too goofy to hold.
And every gust brings a new punchline,
In this forest of charm, everything's fine.

So let's raise a toast to the nonsense we find,
In the vibrant woods, where we laugh uninhibited,
Where whispers and giggles intertwine with grace,
And the secrets we share put smiles on each face!

Melodies Beneath the Canopy

Beneath the leaves, the squirrels play,
They dance and chatter in a cheeky way.
An owl hoots with a comical glare,
While a mouse scampers without a care.

The branches sway, they twist and tease,
A funny breeze brings whispers with ease.
A rabbit hops in a polka dot suit,
As the moonlight giggles, softly astute.

The shadows twirl and leap with glee,
A raccoon winks; oh, such mischief, you see!
With every rustle, a chuckle is spun,
In this leafy stage, laughter's begun.

So join the party, don't be shy,
The woodland creatures will tell you why.
In nature's comedy, we all belong,
Come sway with us to this joyful song!

An Ode to the Wandering Shadows

Shadows danced freely as the sun slipped away,
Playing tricks on the ground in a whimsical fray.
They stretched and contorted in marvelous ways,
Oh, the tales they could tell of the sunniest days.

With a hop and a skip, they paired with the light,
Tickling the toes of a passerby's sight.
They beckoned and waved, those playful dark friends,
With laughter that echoed, their joy never ends.

A cat chased its shadow, a comical show,
While the shadows just giggled, relishing the glow.
They mingled and swayed, in a ballet so grand,
In a dance with the daisies, a whimsical band.

But soon came the night, with a blanket of stars,
The shadows grew sleepy, with visions of Mars.
Yet, just before dreaming, they promised tomorrow,
To return in the daylight, igniting more joy and less sorrow.

Portents of the Shimmering Silk

A spider spun webs with a magical sheen,
As it giggled at flies, 'You'll soon be cuisine!'
With a flick and a flourish, it crafted its lair,
A glistening palace with rooms full of air.

It draped all the silk like a grand tapestry,
While the beetles looked on, what a sight to see!
They whispered and chuckled, 'Is that palace for real?'
As the breeze gave a bow, offering a zeal.

A party ensued in the heart of the glen,
With spiders and bugs showing off now and then.
They twirled and they spun, oh, what a display,
As the moonlight turned gold, washing worries away.

'Watch out for the web!' shouted a cautious old bug,
As a rogue ladybug gave the silk a big hug.
But laughter erupted, what a whimsical kin,
In a world full of silk, let the mischief begin!

Harmonies of the Woodland Choir

In the heart of the woods, where the critters convene,
A chorus of silly birds keep the scene.
They squawk and they squabble, in varying tones,
While the frogs join along, croaking in drones.

A squirrel plays drums on a hollowed-out stump,
As raccoons tap dance, adding a thump.
The owls lend their wisdom, or so they believe,
While the rabbits just hop, "We've got to achieve!"

Their harmonies ripple through branches so wide,
As the sun rays peek through, joining the ride.
Nature's own symphony, played with such flair,
Even the ants form a line in the air.

With laughter and joy, they sing all day long,
In perfect unison, nature's sweet song.
Underneath all the fun, there's a secret they share,
Everyone's welcome, if you dare to care!

Chronicle of the Wandering Breeze

A breeze strolled by with a wiggle and twirl,
It tangled the hair of a passing girl.
She laughed and she danced, what a curious sight,
As the breeze blew along, a mischievous sprite.

It tickled the leaves and flipped over hats,
Started a giggle among the stray cats.
They chased after shadows, both timid and bold,
While the breeze waved goodbye, its laughter untold.

It spun around trees, a playful delight,
Whispered sweet nothings till the moon shone bright.
And all through the night, with a cheeky grin,
The wind kept on frolicking, eager to win.

With a swish and a swoosh, it hummed a tune,
Tickling the flowers beneath the full moon.
A frolicsome dance, the trees swayed in place,
To the whimsical whispers of the grass's embrace.

Lamentation of the Glistening Dew

Morning breaks with a chuckle and cheer,
Dewdrops giggle, absent of fear.
A spider's web, a shimmery veil,
Holds tales of dreams and the whimsy trail.

Grasses tickle the wandering toes,
While blossoms nod, as if to impose.
Dewdrops burst with laughter like jesters,
In this carnival, each gleam is a tester!

A breeze arrives with a playful poke,
Dewdrops dance, burst—oh, what a joke!
Nature's laughter, bright, pure, and bold,
In morning's embrace, there's humor untold!

Sonnet of the Fading Daylight

As sunset yawns, the crickets start,
A symphony played with lively heart.
Fireflies blink like tiny stars,
In twilight's grace, dancing afar.

The moon grins wide, a cheeky chap,
While owls hoot from their twilight nap.
The day's mischief tucks in the light,
What fun is found in the velvet night!

A raccoon stumbles, spills his drink,
In the reeds, frogs pause to think.
Tasked with laughter, through dusk they'll weave,
In this playful night, and none will grieve!

Gaze upon the Dancing Ferns

Ferns sway gently in the breeze,
Waving at flowers: "Don't you sneeze!"
The daisies giggle, twinkling bright,
As petals flutter in sheer delight.

A curious snail takes a quick slide,
Hoping the sunlit paths won't hide.
With each wiggle, he leaves a trace,
An artist's mark, a slimy grace!

Leaves wear the dust of yesterday's sun,
A breezy duet, oh what fun!
Nature spins yarns, both odd and true,
In this sitcom where all things grew!

Rhapsody of the Nature's Heart

In the meadow, rabbits prance,
Chasing shadows, a silly dance.
Butterflies giggle, twirl in flight,
Nature's jesters, what a sight!

Squirrels wear hats made of leaves,
Amidst chaos, the bumblebee weaves.
Trees whisper secrets, roots in a knot,
Who thought they'd quarrel? Not a lot!

Frogs in chorus, croak with flow,
Singing loudly, putting on a show.
Grasshoppers leap, sport tiny grins,
Nature's circus, where laughter begins!

Reverberations in the Glade

In the glade where echoes abound,
Laughter bounces all around.
A fox trips over a hidden log,
Startling a frog who croaks and hogs.

A chorus of giggles from bushes nearby,
As squirrels plot their next daring flyby.
The trees listen in with a rustling sigh,
For they'd tell tales if only they'd try!

A deer poses, then slips on mud,
Creating a splash—a muddy thud!
While rabbits applaud, their ears in the air,
Nature's grand theater, a comedy fair.

Beneath the moon, the fun won't cease,
Even crickets play their tune with ease.
For in the glade, under the stars so bright,
Every rustle and chuckle makes the night light!

The Language of the Quiet Earth

Oh, the gossip from beneath our feet,
Worms spin tales, oh so sweet.
In the soil where secrets lay,
Each dash of rain brings laughter's way.

Mushrooms pop like jokes in the gloom,
They sprout with a giggle, shaking the room.
Pebbles chuckle as they roll on by,
Each one a story, oh my, oh my!

Grass blades wave in a teasing jest,
What do you think? They're the very best!
While the rocks, solemn in their parade,
Act as if they've got nothing to trade.

But behind the scenes, there's a ruckus, a cheer,
For the earth's little creatures hold laughter dear.
In their quiet mess, humor unfurls,
Tales from the ground of our silly world.

Reverie in the Sundrenched Clearing

In the sun where shadows tease,
A dandelion dances with ease.
Its fluff flies away, floaty and free,
A cheeky prank on the bumblebee.

Bees buzz with a whimsical tune,
While a lizard lounges, a lazy cartoon.
A butterfly flutters, oh what a scene,
Wishing on wishes, in shades of green!

The sun winks down, a mischievous ray,
As crickets chirp, in a jazzy ballet.
A nearby tree spills a secret or two,
Whispers of laughter in morning dew.

Among the flowers, a snail moves slow,
With dreams of grandeur, who knows how far they'll go?
But in this clearing, life finds a way,
To giggle and bask in the bright of day!

Soliloquy of the Leafy Knoll

In the grove where gossips play,
Leaves gossip like children at play.
A twig sneezes, birds all clap,
Nature's jest in a leafy cap.

Sunbeams dance on the grass so bright,
A squirrel prances, oh what a sight!
Dropping acorns, he plays the fool,
Who knew that trees could be so cruel?

The wind chuckles, rustles a hat,
A rabbit hops, then flops down flat.
With laughter that fills the empty space,
There's humor hidden in every face.

In the shade, a ladybug twirls,
Making art while the world whirls.
Each leaf a jester in this grand hall,
Nature's circus, inviting all!

Reflections of Soft Echoes

Oh, echoes of laughter bounce off the stream,
Where ducks take a selfie, a charming daydream.
A frog in a bowtie croaks jokes with great flair,
While fish flip their tails in a watery dare.

The sun on the water is playing a prank,
With sparkles and glimmers, it splashes a tank.
Rippled reflections make faces so funny,
While dragonflies giggle, all bright and sunny.

As clouds drift by, wearing hats of fluffy white,
The breeze plays a tune that's light as a kite.
With swans serenading, it's quite the parade,
A jestful embrace in this sparkling glade.

So gather the whispers, let's share in the play,
For laughter and joy light the brightest of days.
Together we swim in the ripples of fun,
In this echoing world, we'll never be done!

Whispers of Beneath the Canopy

Under the tall trees, where vines weave a tale,
The squirrels act out like a furry detail.
A hedgehog in spectacles reads with great flair,
While owls in tuxedos keep watch from midair.

The canopy giggles, it rustles with cheer,
As leaves fall like confetti, let's throw one up here!
Toadstools are serving a tea made of dew,
And mushrooms are laughing, it's all quite the view!

The crickets are chatting about a dance craze,
While fireflies blink in a rhythmic haze.
With lanterns aglow they sway side to side,
In this woodland fiesta, come join for the ride!

As branches weave secrets of whimsical charms,
Nature's comedic play is full of warm arms.
So gather your giggles and dance by the stream,
Let's frolic with whimsy, life's one big dream!

Songs from the Gentle Tide

With waves that are chatty, they dance on the shore,
Shells play the maracas, and seagulls want more.
A crab with a wig struts down by the bay,
While dolphins create their own cabaret play.

The tide hums a tune, it's both sweet and absurd,
Fish wearing sunglasses flap fins to the word.
Mermaids brew coffee, they laugh and they cheer,
While sandy-faced turtles are first in the leer.

Seashells tell stories of oceanic quests,
As jellyfish jiggle, wearing sparkly vests.
A starfish performs with a flip and a flop,
In this underwater carnival, laughter won't stop!

Oh, let's join the fun, bring our giggles and glee,
As crabs start a conga, oh what a sight to see!
With the sun setting low, the tide laughs goodbye,
Sailing home with a chuckle, beneath the pink sky.

Dreamscape of Autumn's Breath

When leaves start to giggle, they dance with delight,
Squirrels wear hats that are silly and bright.
Pumpkins roll by, on their way to a feast,
While acorns debate who will be the least.

Oh, watch as the breeze gives a tickle and tease,
It whispers to branches, and sways through the trees.
A kite with a quack floats high in the sky,
While pie-faces fall, making raccoons cry!

The sun casts its rays in a wobbly bend,
And shadows form creatures that giggle and blend.
As colors explode in a hilarious scheme,
Every step in the park feels like a wild dream.

With hats made of leaves that twirl to the ground,
Nature staged parties, both silly and sound.
So here's to the fun that each autumn can bring,
Let laughter resound, let the cheerful winds sing!

Echoes of the Hidden Glade

In the glade where shadows play,
Mice on stilts come out to sway.
Mushrooms wear hats—what a sight!
Bouncing bunnies join the night.

Echoes chuckle through the trees,
As squirrels juggle acorns with ease.
Lights twinkle like stars in a coat,
While raccoons sing in a silly note.

Crickets and owls form a band,
With beats that make me want to stand.
Hip-hopping deer join the scene,
In this nighttime fun: pure and keen.

The hidden glade, with laughter rife,
Reminds us all of joyous life.
Nature's party never ends,
As every critter makes new friends.

Breath of the Silent Marsh

Marshy whispers float on high,
Reeds gossip beneath the sky.
Crickets chirp in tiny throngs,
Their wild tune sounds like great songs.

Frogs in chorus, holding bets,
Who can leap over the wetsets?
Dragonflies play tag with the breeze,
While turtles smirk at the trees.

"Mud pies!" the piglets squeal with cheer,
I can't wait to have some here.
With plops and splashes, what a mess,
I must admit, I love this dress!

A father heron makes a quip,
"Watch your step, you might just slip!"
But laughter rings and joy unfolds,
In the marsh where silliness holds.

Cadence of the Dancing Limbs

Whimsical trees perform a jig,
While rabbits hop, not too big.
Swaying trunks, a merry tune,
As chipmunks chuckle 'neath the moon.

Twisting branches, a funky beat,
Woodpeckers dance on the bumpy seat.
Breezy whispers tell a tale,
Of broccoli trees and their leafy veil.

Frolicsome shadows prance on ground,
Each leaf and twig hums around.
Nature's merry minstrel song,
Says join the fun; come sing along.

Barking trees, oh what a sight,
As squirrels scamper left and right.
They toss acorns, a silly game,
Nature's version of fame and shame.

Reverie by the Water's Edge

Frogs in tuxedos, croak a tune,
Ducks in top hats strut by noon.
Fish wear goggles, splash with glee,
All invite me for tea by the sea.

The sun is shining, clouds play tag,
Squirrels race with a little brag.
The breeze brings whispers of wild delight,
As I ponder, is that a fish in flight?

Bobbling bubbles dance in air,
Glancing at my silly chair.
Do chairs float or do they sink?
I'll test that out, but first I think.

Giggling willow branches sway,
I shout, "Hey, don't run away!"
Their leaves clatter, "Stay awhile,"
And I can't help but share a smile.

Fireside Murmurs of the Meadow

Beneath the stars, the campfire glows,
Where stories of critters and laughter flows.
A fox tells tales of treasure untold,
As raccoons giggle, their eyes big and bold.

A porcupine strums a twig like a lute,
While bunnies harmonize, oh what a hoot!
The candlelight flickers, shadows take flight,
As squirrels recite poems of whimsy and light.

The owls join in with a wise, deep hoot,
Sharing their secrets, all wrapped in a suit.
Paper lanterns drift softly in night,
As laughter erupts, like bubbles in flight.

In this enchanted circle, joy takes its place,
With friends around fires, the heart finds its pace.
The meadow, a stage, where memories remain,
In whispers and laughter, a delightful refrain.

Voice of the Mystical Glade

In the glade, the ferns start to sway,
As frogs in tuxedos lead the ballet.
Mice in top hats greet the sly fox,
Who winks at the moon while checking his socks.

A bubbling brook spills secrets of fun,
While crickets debate who's the best pun.
Owls are the judges, perched high above,
With feathers and wisdom, they spread the love.

Fireflies glow like little stars near,
As rabbits play hopscotch, never in fear.
With giggles and grins, they jump around,
In this magical space, joy is profound.

Nature conspires to keep spirits bright,
With laughter and legends, it feels just right.
The breeze carries tales of the day,
In this glade where all the critters play.

A Serenade to the Glimmering Heart

A squirrel serenades the night,
With echoing notes that take flight.
While fireflies buzz in glowing dance,
Whispering tales, as if by chance.

A bear in a bowtie, trying to waltz,
Tripping on roots, oh what a fault!
The rabbits chuckle, rolling in glee,
As the clumsy bear aims for a tree.

The wind plays tricks with a tune so sweet,
Tickling the grass, tapping its feet.
With laughter and song, under the stars,
Nature's chorus sings from near and far.

Each rustle, each chuckle, a hint of play,
In this whimsical world, we all long to stay.
With hearts aglow, in its gentle embrace,
Life here feels like a merry race.

Nature's Tranquil Duet

In the meadow, a frog starts to sing,
A soundtrack for bees on the wing.
While squirrels in tuxedos dance around,
In nature's show, joy can be found.

A turtle stuck, trying to spin,
Wobbling and wobbling, oh where to begin?
The blushing flowers giggle with glee,
As the butterfly flirts with the glow of the tree.

Crickets play cards beneath the moon,
While owls misplace all their spoons.
A raccoon joins with a cheeky wink,
And leans on a rock with a slight clink.

Amidst the laughter, the brook starts to flow,
With punchlines and puns hidden below.
In this charming scene, what a delight,
Nature's humor shines, oh what a sight!

Chronicles Beyond the Bark

Past the sturdy trunks, where the playful winds sigh,
Lies a saga outrageous, oh my, oh my!
A beaver in spectacles sketched plans for a dam,
While a hedgehog yelled, "Just wing it, you spam!"

On tiptoe, a hedgehog hid behind a rock,
In hopes of a nibble, a chocolate chip stock.
But a bear stole the treat, with a drowsy-eyed glance,
And soon started a giggle, a big furry dance.

They pranced through the glens, shouting rhymes full of cheer,
Pulling in friends from far and near.
With laughter contagious, they twirled round the oak,
Crafting an evening of jokes that they stoke.

As daylight grew dim, under starry disguise,
They shared tales of mischief, with glint in their eyes.
In chronicles blazing, through bark and through leaf,
Their friendship's the punchline, providing relief.

Lyrics Encased in Oak

Nestled within bark, secrets lie thick,
The whispers of critters, a chorus so quick.
A woodpecker drummer, tapping a beat,
While chipmunks compose, oh, what a treat!

In the shade of the branches, tree spirits collide,
With jokes and banter, their merriment wide.
A turtle in shades tells tales of the past,
Of races he lost but friendships that last.

An owl in a bowtie gave wisdom a spin,
While clever old fox cracked puns with a grin.
The songs encased in oak carried all through the night,
With laughter and joy, their hearts took flight.

At dawn's early blush, when the world starts to wake,
They shared in their stories, no heart left to ache.
From roots to the leaves, every note filled the air,
In a melody bright, like a festival fair.

Cadence of the Flowering Glade

Amidst blooming buds, a rabbit spun round,
With hops and with flops, his joy knew no bound.
A waltz with the daisies, a jig with the breeze,
Sprouting sweet giggles, as light as you please.

A grasshopper strummed on a leaf with finesse,
While bees in their jackets made quite a mess.
They buzzed out a tune, a lively refrain,
Bringing all critters to dance in the rain.

'Round berry bushes, they'd twist and they'd twirl,
A caterpillar spun like a golden girl.
Each twist brought a laugh, each turn was a cheer,
In the flowering glade, where humor drew near.

As night wrapped its blanket and stars came to play,
They swayed to the rhythm of twilight's ballet.
With the moon's gentle glow and soft whispers so sweet,
Their cadence of joy made every heart beat.

The Diary of Shaded Journeys

In a shady nook, where giggles bloom,
A squirrel named Dave danced like a cartoon.
Bumbled through leaves, tripped on a twig,
Chasing a butterfly, feeling quite big.

A frog in a tie played hopscotch with glee,
While a raccoon critiqued his fine symmetry.
They sang to the sky, a most curious cheer,
Echoing laughter that all could hear.

A parrot perched high, spouting pure jest,
While critters below tried to mimic the best.
With each splashy flap and wiggle of tail,
A riot of fun like a whimsical tale.

At day's end, they gathered 'neath branches so wide,
Swapping their stories with big grins of pride.
In the diary of laughter, they sketched every scene,
Doodling their dreams in the shade, oh so green.

The Spirit of the Serene Hollow

In the peaceful hollow, spirits delight,
With giggles that echo, a joyful sight.
The sunbeams peek through leafy crowns,
While chipmunks scurry in little gowns.

A turtle slow dances, unsure of his feet,
While frogs in tuxedos enjoy their beats.
The tall grass sways, a gentle push,
As rabbits hop in with a blushing bush.

The laughter of leaves fills the air,
As wise old owls spin tales with flair.
Fireflies twinkle, casting their glow,
While bathtubs of dew bring silliness slow.

So here in this hollow, peace intertwines,
With humor woven in nature's designs.
The spirit of laughter, calm, yet bright,
In the serene hollow, everything's right.

An Overture to the Fluttering Wings

Butterflies don capes of glee,
As they flutter 'round a jolly tree.
Birds chirp laugh tracks on repeat,
In this overture of fun so sweet.

The dragonflies zoom like race cars,
Bumping into leaves, dodging stars.
A buzzing bee cracks a joke aloud,
Sending the blossoms into a crowd.

Playful winds start a merry chase,
Sending leaves whirling in a dainty race.
The frogs join in with corny tunes,
Winking at crickets, beneath the moons.

Laughter carried on brightened wings,
Nature's symphony, oh how it sings!
An overture of joyful flight,
In a lighthearted, whimsical night.

Symphony of the Hallowed Woods

In the woods where the critters sing,
A notable laugh is the real king.
The branches sway, conducting cheer,
While chipmunks chirp their plans so clear.

A raccoon, quite dapper in style,
Steals snacks, then grins with great guile.
The trees shake their leaves, a gentle sigh,
As the nearby pond reflects the sky.

Dancing shadows in gleeful fits,
Squirrels heckle with quick little skits.
The air is filled with joking glee,
From even the grumpiest tree.

Under the moon's giggling light,
Nature's party feels just right.
A symphony of giggles and grins,
In the hallowed woods, the fun begins.

The Enchanted Tones of Evening

In the grove where squirrels play,
The trees join in quite a fray.
A breeze whispers secrets so sweet,
While crickets tap dance on their feet.

Owls hoot out their nightly jests,
Playing games like furry pests.
Raccoons wear masks like they're cool,
Who knew the woods had such a school?

The stars blink, a twinkling tease,
As fireflies buzz beneath the leaves.
Bunny hops with a comic flair,
As clumsy foxes fumble and stare.

So join the fun in this wild spot,
Where laughter echoes, a friendly lot.
Evening tunes twist and twirl,
In nature's comedy, whirls and swirls.

Echoes in the Breeze

The whispering winds carry a jest,
With giggling leaves, they do their best.
A donkey croaks out rhymes so strange,
While butterflies dance in joyful range.

A dandelion tickles the sky,
As puffy seeds take off to fly.
With poofs and puffs, they spread their cheer,
In a lighthearted flight, oh dear!

The sunbeams wink with golden beams,
As squirrels giggle, caught in dreams.
With every rustle, laughter grows,
As whispers play where the wild wind blows.

In this realm where humor flows,
Nature's joy is all that shows.
Each chuckle shared beneath the trees,
Is a melody carried in the breeze.

The Arcane Tune of Nature's Heart

A woodpecker taps out a beat,
On tree bark, oh what a treat!
The ants form lines, they march in style,
Wiggling their bums, they go a mile.

A wise old owl, with glasses perched,
Explains why worms can't be church.
With feathery jokes from dusk till dawn,
His chuckles wake the sleepy fawn.

A brook giggles over smooth stones,
It splashes all while sharing puns.
The shadows dance, the shadows play,
As nature hums a cheeky sway.

From chirps to hums, sweet sounds ignite,
The forest sparkles, pure delight.
In laughter's grip, the day is sweet,
With every critter on their feet.

Enchantment in the Verdant Veil

Under leaves of emerald sheen,
A chipmunk twirls, he's quite the scene.
He tells of cheese and endless pies,
As ladybugs giggle, rolling eyes.

The vines hold secrets, hum and hum,
While froggies hop to a polka drum.
They leap and dance on lily pads,
In this green realm, all woes are bad.

A flower winks with petals bright,
And twirls her colors, pure delight.
With every bloom a chuckle sounds,
As whispers float in joyful rounds.

The magic here, it tickles pink,
As critters chat and roses wink.
In leafy laughter, all abide,
Where mirth and mirthful hearts reside.

Storyteller's Echo in the Wild

In the woods where critters roam,
A rabbit wears a cozy comb.
He brushes fur from ear to foot,
And sings to trees with roots so cute.

A squirrel quips about the rain,
His acorn hat is quite insane.
With every drop, he shimmies down,
And twirls around in puddles brown.

A fox recites bizarre old tales,
Of talking shells and dancing snails.
The other beasts just laugh and cheer,
As trees sway gently, lending ear.

Each laugh echoes, a joyful sound,
In this delightful, grassy ground.
The forest thrives with silly sights,
As stories wing on breezy nights.

Chorus of the Enchanted Thicket

In a thicket where shadows blend,
The raccoons plot, they won't pretend.
With noodle arms and silly masks,
They dance around while nature basks.

A hedgehog plays a tiny drum,
While everyone joins in the hum.
The trees sway, with leafy guffaws,
Every branch a whimsical cause.

A lizard hops on a toad's hat,
And they compete on who's more fat.
The moon grins wide, its face aglow,
As the night teems with humor's flow.

With every rustle, peace is made,
In the laughter, worries fade.
Together under the night's embrace,
In this enchanted, jolly place.

Soundtrack of Sunlit Days

A bee buzzes with grand delight,
Searching blooms in the warm sunlight.
A mouse in shades, quite the trend,
Rumbling around, just to offend.

Birds with voices, a wonderful din,
Composing an anthem to grin.
Each twig snapping, it's a show,
As the earth chuckles, soft and low.

The sunball rolls across the sky,
And bumbles by with a silly sigh.
Grasshoppers leap with perfect flair,
While a snail slowly makes its dare.

In this merry, sunlit play,
The flowers prance, hip-hip-hooray!
Laughter echoes in the sway,
Creating joy in bright display.

Whispers of the Timeworn Trees

Beneath the boughs, a secret sigh,
Old tales of owls and a pie.
The squirrels gossip, tails in a knot,
While a wise old tortoise just forgot.

Crickets wink, a cheeky bunch,
Sharing snacks for a twilight lunch.
Only a mole sees the joke,
As he chuckles beneath the oak.

A parrot squawks, oh what a tease,
Claiming he can mimic the breeze.
With every rustle, the woods ignite,
As laughter spills into the night.

In the dance of dusk's gentle rays,
The trees giggle in playful ways.
From roots to crowns, humor runs free,
A riddle wrapped in greenery.

Rhapsody in the Golden Light

In the meadow, squirrels dance,
Shaking nuts with every prance.
A butterfly steals the show,
While daisies sway to and fro.

Chasing shadows, they all play,
In a most peculiar way.
A frog croaks a laugh so loud,
Making even thistles proud.

A rabbit hops, a spin so bold,
Telling tales of carrots old.
The sun dips low, sings its tune,
As crickets join, a goofy croon.

Laughing leaves, oh what a sight!
Tickling branches, full of light.
Nature's giggles fill the air,
In a world of whimsical flair.

Echoing Dreams of the Dappled Light

Sunshine dances in a patchwork array,
Each beam casting shadows that giggle and play.
With whispers of wishes, they twirl in delight,
Beneath the bright canopy, they frolic in flight.

A donkey's bray joins the merry parade,
Echoing loud, making moments cascade.
Ducks don their sunglasses, a sight quite absurd,
As they waddle in line, chatter and chirp heard.

Butterflies don fancy coats, oh what a flair!
Flitting and fluttering without a care.
They tease the flowers with their colorful dance,
While dappled light glimmers, creating a trance.

In these echoing dreams, clowns take a bow,
With jests and antics, they make us avow.
Laughter drifts freely in the soft, warm air,
In a world of delight, oh how we declare!

Haunting Tones of the Still Air

Whispers of leaves dance, spooky yet bright,
Telling tales of ghouls in the night.
The owl hoots, "What's that ruckus?"
While bats swoop down, all in focus.

A ghostly breeze with a ticklish sigh,
Rustles the tales that flutter by.
Mice dream of cheese, oh what a fright,
While shadows chuckle at their delight.

In moonlit glades, the laughter roams,
With echoes that tease when the night condones.
Boo! A cat jumps, with a playful pout,
In the haunting tones, there's no room for doubt.

But come dawn, the stories lay bare,
Sunrise shines on the night's wild affair.
Bets are placed on who'll go bump,
In the still air, a whimsical thump.

Breath of the Serene Wilderness

A breeze stirs up a playful song,
Nature's orchestra, all day long.
Birds in tutus, dancing with flair,
Chirping their notes in comedic air.

The brook bubbles, "Hey, watch me slip!"
As frogs ribbit in a wibbly blip.
Grasshoppers leap and then get stuck,
In the sticky sap of a hapless luck.

Bumblebees buzz with a zany hum,
Gathering nectar, oh what fun!
A racoon runs in with a silly grin,
Waving goodbye as it jumps in.

Even the sun wears a goofy hat,
And chuckles softly at this and that.
In wilderness serenades, giggles flow,
With every rustle, a funny show.

Chronicles of the Swaying Cypress

In the breeze, the trees do dance,
Spinning tales with each goofy prance.
Squirrels laugh, hiding from the view,
While the branches shake, playing peekaboo.

As leaves toss hats, like the garden's jest,
A branch swings low, it's quite the quest.
In a game of tag, they join the fun,
Even the gnomes cheer for the sun!

Roots tickle toes, a tickle fight,
Cypress chortles under twilight.
A wind-driven joke, so merry and spry,
Leaving all to giggle and sigh.

When shadows lengthen, the yarns grow tall,
Echoes of laughter stir all in all.
A cypress conclave, a festival grand,
Hilarity sprouts from nature's hand.

Tides of Twilight Whispers

As twilight slips upon the scene so bright,
Fireflies conference, their lanterns ignite.
They gossip of moons and their silver glow,
While crickets provide the beat, a lively show.

Rabbits wear shoes made of thistle and thread,
Stomping to rhythms until they dread.
The lullaby of night fills the air,
With owls spinning tales of fluff and flair.

Stars twinkle back like they share in the fun,
And mist wanders by like a sneak with a run.
The river chuckles as it trickles away,
Drawing doodles on shores, oh what a play!

Clouds become pillows, bunnies take flight,
In this night so tender, all worries feel light.
With giggles and whispers, the world's softly bright,
Twilight's a jester, oh what a night!

Floatation of Fall's Embrace

Leaves twirl and swirl like a dervish in glee,
Frolicking down from their branches with spree.
Pumpkins giggle as they roll in the patch,
While scarecrows strut with a flimsy mustache.

The acorns are plotting their tricks with a pluck,
Creating a ruckus, oh you're in for a luck!
Squirrels spin tales like acrobats bold,
Each leap an adventure, a treasure to hold.

Breezes whisper secrets in playful delight,
As shadows and sunlight have a whimsical fight.
A waltz of the leaves in their colorful dress,
Tickling the earth, oh what a mess!

The season wears laughter wrapped up in delight,
As critters in hats have a grand old night.
Tick-tocking time with a giggle or two,
In this festival of fall, there's fun born anew!

Reveries in the Shelter of Bark

Under the canopy, the critters conspire,
A chorus of giggles shot up like a fire.
Raccoons play poker with a deck of leaves,
While chatty chipmunks spin tall tales like thieves.

A tree stump with sass claims it's the king,
While worms worm their way into gossip and fling.
A crow with a monocle speaks of the past,
Dreaming of moments that flew by too fast.

The sun comes by dressed up in gold,
Telling tales of adventures both brave and bold.
The shadows mimicking every bold stance,
Tempting the wind into a whimsical dance.

Nature's pranks combine with delight,
Each twist and turn brings laughter in flight.
From rabbits in suits to owls with bling,
In this world of whimsy, let the fun ring!

Songs Carried on the Wind

There once was a breeze so spry,
It tickled the leaves as they danced high.
Birds burst out laughing in the trees,
Chasing their shadows with a teasing breeze.

Squirrels with acorns played a tune,
While bumping their heads like a cartoon.
The grass giggled under the sun,
As butterflies joined in on the fun.

Once a feather caught a ride,
It bounced on the air, oh what a glide!
It dropped on a snail, who let out a cheer,
Together they laughed, squinting at deer.

Then came the frogs in a fine parade,
With tiny top hats and serenades.
They croaked out jests, oh what a show,
The world was a stage, just watch it go!

Tales from the Gentle Wind

The breeze carries stories, soft as a sigh,
Of hiccuping trees and silly clouds passing by.
A whisper of laughter follows each gust,
As dandelions tumble, oh, what a fuss!

The wind chats with flowers, a friendly exchange,
"Your colors are wild, but I think they're strange!"
They giggle and sway, each in their place,
While moths draw mustaches, what a funny face!

A bee makes a blunder, gets stuck in a bloom,
As petals start tickling, oh how they zoom!
The sun tries to hide under puffs of gray,
But giggles escape, it can't keep away!

The wind swoops down, with tales it bestows,
Whirling and twirling, where humor just flows.
In this windy world, each twist tells a tale,
Nature's own laughter, in every inhale!

Harmony of the Waving Grasses

In fields of green, the grasses unite,
Each blade a dancer in the moonlight.
They sway to the rhythm of whispers so sweet,
While bugs bop along to a tiny beat.

A rabbit prances with ears all akimbo,
He hops to the left; then he zips like a limbo.
The wind giggles, tickling each fellow,
As daisies chime in, oh so mellow!

The sunset paints hues with laughter and glee,
Making shadows all twist like giddy spaghetti.
A twirling scorpion flies by wearing shades,
Fashion failure? Oh, those are the grades!

Nature applauds with rustling sound,
While critters conclude their frolic abound.
In waving grasses, you'll find pure delight,
A funny symphony under the night!

Dance of the Twilit Shadows

In the dusk, the shadows start to waltz,
With twirling figures, no collars or faults.
A frog jumps in, a pirouette grand,
Till he trips on a root, oh what a stand!

Grass blades giggle, tickling the toes,
While crickets compose the tune that flows.
A firefly blinks in sync with the beat,
Its glow spoiling shadows' tap dancing feat!

The moon rolls in, takes a bow and smiles,
While owls wink, sharing laughter for miles.
Every creature joins, a comical spree,
In twilight's embrace, wild and carefree!

With each shuffle, the night sings loud,
As low-hanging branches form a crowd.
Nature's own stage, where absurd truly reigns,
This dance of delight, where whimsy remains!

Murmurs Beneath the Branches

In a forest, the leaves gossip loud,
Squirrels dance, putting on a show proud.
They leap and twirl with acorn in hand,
While branches chuckle, oh isn't it grand!

A rabbit hops, slips, creates quite a mess,
With a flip and a flop, he's got no finesse.
Birds drop twigs like confetti from above,
Sharing their secrets, their laughter, their love.

The wind joins in, a giggling spree,
Whispering jokes 'bout the buzzing bee.
The sun shines down, a spotlight so bright,
As nature's circus plays day and night!

Oh, the antics beneath the tall trees,
Where mischief blossoms carried by breeze.
Humor in every rustle and grin,
Nature's own jesters, let the fun begin!

Serenade of the Shivering Branches

Branches shake and shimmy about,
Creating rhythms, no doubt!
A woodpecker's knock, a tap dance spree,
Squirrels join in, filled with glee.

The trees quiver in playful jest,
Singing out loud, a true fest.
Acorns drop like confetti flakes,
As branches cheer with little shakes.

A bunny hops in the moon's cool glow,
Fumbles dancing, stole the show!
Vines swing low, swaying for fun,
And the night laughs with each clever pun.

Branches serenade the sleepy night,
In their jive, everything feels right.
Nature's melodies, so sweet and grand,
With funny echoes that softly stand.

Songs of the Gentle Wind

The gentle wind hums a song,
Teasing bobbing heads along.
It whips the grass with a cheeky grin,
While butterflies twirl, a whimsical spin.

A dandelion giggles in the breeze,
Blowing puffs with elegant ease.
"Catch me if you can!" it gleefully shouts,
As birds break out in joyful flouts.

Clouds pass by with a knowing wink,
"Watch out for storms!" they slyly think.
But the sun shines bright, a cheeky chap,
Keeping everyone in some kind of flap.

In the field where laughter flows,
Windy tunes nobody knows.
In every gust, a chuckle found,
Songs of the wind, so merry, so sound.

Harmony of the Rustling Leaves

Leaves rustle softly, tickling ears,
Whispers of secrets, laughter nears.
A squirrel sings a silly tune,
To the rhythm of a sleepy moon.

Branches sway like dancers free,
Bumbling bunnies join in glee.
Trees gossip with a wobbly breeze,
Footsteps follow with wobbly knees.

Melodies played on bark so old,
Stories of mischief yet untold.
A leaf falls down, a grand parade,
Nature's jesters, all afraid!

Echoes echo off the hills,
Frolicking creatures, all the thrills.
In harmony, a funny show,
The rustling leaves put on a glow.

Lullabies in the Twilight Grove

In the grove where shadows play,
Squirrels dance both night and day.
Chasing tails and giggles bright,
Owls hoot jokes beneath moonlight.

Fireflies twinkle in a race,
Frogs croak laughter, what a face!
Whispers swirl in gentle breeze,
Nature's pranks put minds at ease.

A raccoon sneaks a midnight snack,
While rabbits hop in twos, not slack.
Branches sway, a comical sight,
Mice tumble down, oh what a fright!

So close your eyes, let dreams take flight,
In twilight's grove, not a worry in sight.
Lullabies sung by nature's crew,
As giggles echo beneath the dew.

Dreamweaver's Call in the Grove

In the grove where dreams take flight,
A frog croaks softly, his timing just right.
With stars in his eyes, he leaps for a note,
While fireflies giggle, aloft like a boat.

A rabbit recites lines from a past laughter,
Of cakes made of carrots and jelly thereafter.
Laughter ripples through the shimmering veil,
As echoes of giggles ride on the trail.

Soliloquy in the Shade

In the cool shade, a mouse takes a seat,
With a cup of acorn tea, oh what a treat!
He debates life's meaning with a wise old ant,
While hatching a scheme for a grand, tiny plant.

A bee buzzes in, wearing tiny specs,
Laughing at tales of the neighborly wrecks.
The sun's rays join, adding to the play,
As all join the fun on this glorious day.

Resonance of the Dappled Sun

Under leaves where laughter springs,
A squirrel juggles acorns, oh what funny things!
Sunshine tickles with a golden hand,
While shadows shimmy, oh, isn't it grand?

Butterflies flutter, a colorful crew,
They stop for a chat, as if asking "Who?"
A nearby tree chuckles, roots deep in cheer,
It sways with the breeze, whispering 'You're here!'

Songs Carried on Gentle Tides

In the breeze, I lost my hat,
It danced like a bird, quite round and fat.
A fish winked at me, made quite a scene,
While seagulls debated the best place to preen.

A crab wore my shoe, thinking it grand,
As waves played tag with the soft, warm sand.
The sun chuckled low, a mischievous flame,
And the tide sang out, calling my name.

The Gaze of the Starry Veil

Under a sky with stars aglow,
An owl wears specs, taking it slow.
He hoots and laughs, a sight to see,
Sipping moonlight, sipping glee.

A hedgehog twirls with a playful grin,
While fireflies join in, hoping to win.
They flash their lights, a glowing dance,
While crickets take their chance to prance.

A bunny dreams of a chocolate pie,
While the stars above wink as they fly.
Frogs leap high, but land in a splash,
Creating ripples of giggles in a flash.

And as the night wears its silvery shawl,
Nature sings softly, enthralling all.
In this whimsical dance of night,
The gazes turn funny, pure delight.

Nursery Rhymes of Nature

Two little bees buzz around a bloom,
Playing hide-and-seek, in their sweet room.
One shouts, "Buzz off!" but can't hide well,
While daisies giggle, casting their spell.

A playful breeze tickles the grass,
As ants in shoes waddling pass.
They trip and tumble, oh what a sight,
With nothing but joy, they take flight!

A spider spinning tales of grand,
Weaving laughter with each little strand.
He shimmies up to take a bow,
Painting the sun with a sunny vow.

The rhymes of nature are sung aloud,
As all the critters gather the crowd.
In this joyful play, no room for grump,
Just laughter and fun in every thump!

Ballad of the Hidden Springs

Beneath a rock, a mouse does hide,
With a treasure map — what a wild ride!
He squeaks and laughs, it leads to cake,
Concealed where no one dares to take.

The weasels plan a noisy feast,
While hedgehogs argue, 'Not the least!'
A family of ducks quack with cheer,
Trying to figure out who's near.

A turtle runs a marathon slow,
But all the frogs just jump and show.
"Oh come on, don't be a glum!
Just join us for a merry hum!"

And as the sun dips low in the sky,
A splash of water makes friends fly.
Together they cheer, to springs they cling,
In this merry dance, let the laughter ring!

The Voice of the Rustling Underbrush

A squirrel in a funny hat,
Dances with a playful rat.
They giggle as they ride a breeze,
Tickling leaves like silly tease.

A frog with glasses reads a book,
While snails take time to stop and look.
A chatterbird sings out a tune,
Making flowers laugh 'neath the moon.

A rabbit hops in fuzzy shoes,
Telling tales of wild blue hues.
The bushes rustle with delight,
As nature dances through the night.

And in the dark, a glowworm winks,
While tree trunks share their laughing jinks.
Together they jest, they whir and sway,
In the underbrush, where fun holds sway.

The Play of Light Between the Leaves

Sunbeams peeked through the leafy dance,
Creating shadows with a playful glance,
A chipmunk pranced in a sunlight patch,
His antics bright, quite the lively match!

The leaves rustled, a playful tease,
Whispering secrets in the gentle breeze,
Every flicker, a pulse of cheer,
As sunlight played, drawing us near!

The branches jiggled, a joyous crew,
Clapping hands, as if they knew,
A forest party in the making,
With laughter sparkling, joy awaking!

So join the dance, feel the thrill,
In the play of light, we find our fill,
With shadows twisting, smiles aglow,
A whimsical world where merriment flows!

Chords of the Blushing Blooms

Petals flutter, colors clash,
Sunflowers wink, blooms do a splash,
A bee buzzed by with a cheeky tune,
Tap dancing softly, under the moon!

Tulips whispered to roses bright,
"Tickle my stems, it feels just right!"
Laughter echoed through the air,
As butterflies danced without a care!

The jasmine giggled, tangled in glee,
Spreading aroma, come smell me!
With laughter ringing in every stitch,
Nature's patch just had a rich pitch!

So join the chorus, give a cheer,
In the garden, there's nothing to fear,
For every bloom, a tale unfurls,
In chords of laughter, nature swirls!

The Quietude of Verdant Echos

In the meadow, a frog took the stage,
Croaking jokes, he earned his wage,
The daisies giggled, they couldn't hold,
Their petals shook, a sight to behold!

A rabbit hopped with quite the flair,
Wore a top hat, oh debonair,
With a bow and a silly dance,
Inviting all for a merry chance!

The whispers rustled, secrets shared,
With every tickle, no one cared,
A breeze laughed by, in fits and starts,
Tickling buds and silly hearts!

So listen close, the echoes play,
In verdant fields, where laughter stays,
Amidst the green, a fun parade,
A whimsical world, where joy is made!

Harmonies of the Autumn Wind

The leaves were dancing with a flair,
A squirrel joined, without a care,
He spun and twirled, a daring show,
While acorns bounced, oh what a flow!

The wind, it chuckled, quite amused,
As branches swayed, all bemused,
The sun peeked in, a sneaky grin,
While nature laughed, let the fun begin!

From high on branches, chatter rose,
A robin's song wore a silly pose,
Chasing shadows, they slipped and slid,
It's a festival where nobody hid!

So gather round, enjoy the spree,
The autumn's laugh, as bold as can be,
In every gust, a comic gem,
Nature's joke gets a hearty stem!

Notes from Nature's Embrace

Birds chirp quips in joyous flight,
Making each other laugh with might.
A nut fell down with quite a plop,
While raccoons dance and never stop!

Puddles giggle at a passing duck,
Splashing happily, oh what luck!
Nature's music is bright and bold,
Tickling our hearts as stories unfold!

Chimes of the Cultivated Grasses

Grasses sing a happy tune,
Swaying with the afternoon.
A rabbit joins; it hops along,
Trying to fit in, but goes all wrong!

Each clump of green can't keep still,
They tickle toes, oh what a thrill!
Dandelions join the choir,
Singing loudly, never tire!

Ballad of the Wandering Shadows

Shadows prance on ground so light,
Playing tag from day to night.
One trips over a rocky stone,
And whispers, 'Oh, I'm all alone!'

They twirl and spin, then take a bow,
Every step, a giggly vow.
But when the sun decides to hide,
They all collide, what a silly ride!

Tones of the Quivering Trunks

In the breeze, the trees do sway,
A dance that wouldn't last a day.
Branches giggle, leaves they laugh,
What a silly tree, oh what a gaffe!

Roots are tickled by little ants,
Doing the conga in their tiny pants.
Bark keeps cracking jokes, it's true,
While squirrels plot a comedy cue!

Grace Notes of the Forest Floor

Underneath the olive trees,
A rabbit tickles a buzzing bee.
They share a joke, a funny pun,
While the daisies sway, oh what fun!

Chipmunks juggle acorns high,
While butterflies flirt as they fly by.
A snail slowly winks with glee,
Claiming he's the fastest one you'll see.

The old oak whispers tales of cheer,
Of past mischief that wanders near.
A crow caws loud, with flair and style,
Challenging all to join his mile.

In the bushes, a squirrel plays chess,
Against a mouse in a tiny dress.
With laughter ringing through the trees,
Nature's orchestra plays with ease.

Chronicles of Nature's Murmurs

In the grove where the critters dance,
A raccoon wears a bright blue pants.
He twirls about with such great flair,
While squirrels gossip without a care.

The bees buzz jokes in their tiny hive,
While ants march on like they're all alive.
Each leaf a stage for a jest so grand,
Nature's laughter throughout the land.

A turtle slides with style and grace,
Looking quite dapper, oh what a face!
He nods to the frog who croaks in rhyme,
Claiming next week will be his prime time.

With a sly grin, the owl looks down,
In his spectacles, he wears a crown.
"Whooo's the funniest?" he hoots aloud,
The forest giggles, so proud, so proud.

Secrets of the Rustling Canopy

High up, secrets rustle with flair,
As critters gossip, unaware.
Breezes tickle the leafy tips,
A chuckle here, a giggle slips.

Sunlight winks on the leafy crowd,
As branches sway, they're feeling proud.
Nature's banter, a funny riddle,
In a symphony, they love to fiddle.

Serenade of the Swaying Boughs

Boughs sway to a tune so bright,
Teasing crows and swiping flight.
A lesson learned from the bending trees,
To dance in pairs, oh, what a tease!

Chirping birds join the lively cheer,
While squirrels hold a grand career.
A waltz of branches, a clumsy spree,
Nature's laughter, wild and free.

Song of the Whispering Leaves

Leaves chatter secrets, in the breeze,
Frogs croak back with squeaky tease.
One leaf whispers, it's quite obscene,
The way they shimmy, a leafy scene.

Butterflies laugh, they twirl with glee,
While ants march in, a wobbly spree.
It's a parade, a silly show,
As whispers twirl in the sunlight's glow.

Lament of the Gnarled Trees

Gnarled limbs bend with a creak,
Squirrels laugh, it's all a sneak.
Their knots dance but no one cares,
Twisted jokes float in the air.

Raccoons giggle at the sight,
Who knew bark could spark such light?
Their jokes are old, they never fade,
While wise old trunks just roll in shade.

Parting Mist and Rising Dawn

As morning breaks with coffee beans,
The squirrels sip on leafy greens.
They gossip soft, their tails a swish,
While rabbits ponder today's big fish.

A dandelion, with dreams held tight,
Blows its seeds into the light.
On dewy grass, they twirl and spin,
With giggles born from dust and gin.

Treetop Tales of Ancient Dreams

In a treehouse high, the parrots squawk,
Sharing secrets, a feathered talk.
Old turtles waddle, a slow parade,
Telling tales of mischief made.

With acorns tossed, they play charades,
Mice join in, their antics displayed.
Every branch a stage for fun,
Under the light of the setting sun.

Hymn of the Chestnut Paths

On tangled trails where giggles roam,
A hedgehog hums his welcome home.
With pricky friends, they plan a feast,
    Of acorn pie—a nutty beast!

They juggle shells and trip on roots,
While bunnies skate in tiny boots.
Chestnuts roll, a bumpy ride,
A parade of joy, side by side!

Duet of Moonlit Reflections

Beneath the stars, a raccoon sings,
In a top hat made of twigs and strings.
He winks at owls, who hoot with glee,
As squirrels dance by, a sight to see.

A frog in slippers leaps with grace,
While fireflies twirl, a glowing race.
The pond's a stage for antics grand,
Nature's laughter, a joyful band.

Original title:
The Whistle of Willows

Copyright © 2025 Creative Arts Management OÜ
All rights reserved.

Author: Jameson Hartfield
ISBN HARDBACK: 978-1-80567-197-8
ISBN PAPERBACK: 978-1-80567-496-2

www.ingramcontent.com/pod-product-compliance
Lightning Source LLC
Chambersburg PA
CBHW071853160426
43209CB00003B/531